# BRAIN ACADEMY
## Quests

MISSION
FILE 2

Penny Hollander,
Jenny Plastow,
Louise Moore and
Richard Cooper

Consultant for NACE:
Sue Mordecai

nace

RISING STARS

**Rising Stars** are grateful to the following people
for their support in developing this series:
Julie Fitzpatrick, Johanna Raffan and Belle Wallace

**nace**

NACE, PO Box 242, Arnolds Way, Oxford, OX2 9FR
www.nace.co.uk

Rising Stars UK Ltd, 22 Grafton Street, London W1S 4EX
www.risingstars-uk.com

Published 2005
Text, design and layout © Rising Stars UK Ltd

Editorial Consultant: Sue Mordecai
Design: Hart McLeod
Illustrations: Cover and insides – Sue Lee / Characters – Bill Greenhead
Cover Design: Burville-Riley

British Library Cataloguing in Publication Data.
A CIP record for this book is available from the British Library.

ISBN: 1-905056-33-8

Printed by Vincenzo Bona, Turin

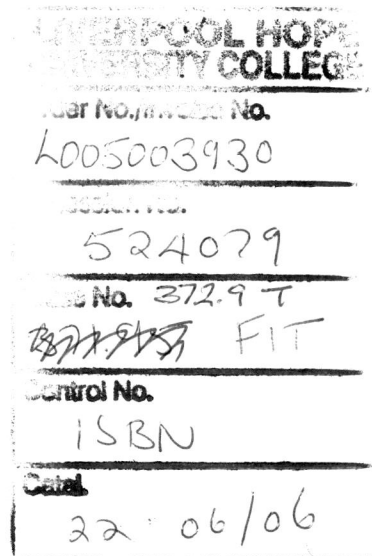

# CONTENTS

# Welcome to Brain Academy!

> Welcome to Brain Academy. Make yourself at home. This section is all about the Academy.

> We are going to help Da Vinci and his friends complete the quests. We would like you to help us. Are you up to the challenge?

## Da Vinci
Da Vinci is the head of the Brain Academy. He is possibly the cleverest person alive. He communicates through a computer. He will set the quests.

## Huxley
Huxley is Da Vinci's right-hand man. He is not quite as clever but very smart. Huxley is cool under pressure.

## Dr Hood
The mad doctor is the arch-enemy of Da Vinci. He and his DAFT (Dull And Feeble Thinkers) agents will do anything they can to annoy the good people of this planet.

## Hilary Kumar
Ms Kumar is the Prime Minister of our country. She will only call the Brain Academy in an extreme emergency. She is confident and strong willed.

## General Cods-Wallop
This decorated (with medals not wallpaper) gentleman is in charge of the armed forces. Da Vinci has to help him out of lots of scrapes.

## Mrs Tiggles
Stella Tiggles is the retired head of the Secret Intelligence Service. Mrs Tiggles' faithful friend is her cat, Bond… James Bond.

We were just like you once — ordinary children leading ordinary lives. Then we received a call from Da Vinci and became secret members of Brain Academy.

Here are a few things you should know about the people you will meet on the journey.

## Echo the Eco-Warrior
Echo loves nature and will do anything to help the environment – even if it means she is going to get her clothes dirty.

## Maryland T Wordsworth
M T Wordsworth is the President of the USA. He likes to be known as Tex and not Mary.

## Buster Crimes
Buster is a really cool dude and is in charge of the Police Force. He is always outwitting Dr Hood and his DAFT agents.

## Serena
Serena is a new character to Brain Academy. A time-traveller, Serena knows all about what went on before – and a bit about the future too.

## Sandy Buckett
The fearless Sandy Buckett is the head of the Fire Service. Sandy and her team of brave firefighters are always on hand, whether to extinguish the flames of chaos caused by the demented Dr Hood or just to rescue Mrs Tiggles' cat.

## Victor Blastov
Victor is a space scientist but struggles with science. Often it is Brain Academy who has to help him get things off the ground.

## Prince Barrington
Prince Barrington is the publicity-seeking heir to the throne. Bazza, as he likes to be known, is always helping out good causes.

# Working with Brain Academy

Do you get the idea? Now you've had the introduction we are going to show you the best way to use this book.

## The Quest

This tells you what the quest is about.

## Research Area

Da Vinci will give you some research tips before you start working on the brief.

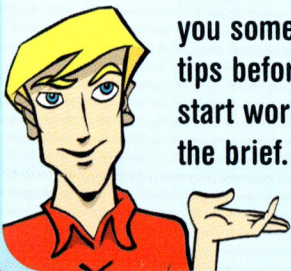

### Hedgehog Alert!

An amazing fact, Huxley! Hedgehogs form 29% of mammals killed on British roads each year.

That's a disaster for our prickly pals, Da Vinci. What can we do to help?

I know, we'll launch a 'Hedgehog Alert' campaign!

#### The Quest

Questers, the Academy is near a busy main road and there have been several sightings recently of dead hedgehogs close by. You are going to start a campaign alerting people to the dangers for hedgehogs. You will need to advise everyone of the basic facts about hedgehog welfare and organisations that can help.

STOP

#### Research Area

Start your research here:
http://www.software-technics.com/bhps/carers.html

There is more information on pages 46–47.

32

Each mission is divided up into different parts.

No one said this was easy. In fact that is why you have been chosen. Da Vinci will only take the best and he believes that includes you. Good luck!

Each book contains a number of 'quests' for you to take part in. You will work with the characters in Brain Academy to complete these quests.

## The Brief

This is where you try to complete the challenge.

## The Brief

Your fact-file will need to include the essential information about where hedgehogs live and what they eat. You will then need to provide information about:
- the daily risks that hedgehogs face;
- different organisations that exist to help in the preservation of hedgehogs;
- how individuals can help.

Remember that a campaign needs eye-catching material as well as factual information, so you could include:
- a slogan or logo on advertising material for a poster or badge;
- pictures from the internet.

Remember to divide your information into clear sections and make it easy and interesting to read so that people will be persuaded to help.

Use bullet points too; they get the info across and are quick to read!

## Da Vinci Files

Well done! Now design a small wildlife area for our Brain Academy which will both attract hedgehogs and provide a safe environment for them. Show your designs on an eye-catching poster to put up in the school hall.

33

## Da Vinci Files

These problems are for the best Brain Academy recruits. Very tough. Are you tough enough?

PS: See pages 44—47 for a useful process and hints and tips!

# Sculpture vulture

*If someone makes a big sculpture, where could it go for people to see it?*

*Can you find out where I could go to see some?*

*Sometimes they are in shopping centres! But lots of countries have parks for big sculptures.*

## The Quest

Your quest is to make an information booklet for Da Vinci. He doesn't know much about sculpture, so you will need to show him some different artists' work.

## Research Area

Try this site to find out about sculpture:

http://www.nelson-atkins.org/sculpture/henrymoore/moore1.htm
http://www.fortunecity.com/westwood/arch/769/Vigeland/

There is more information on pages 46–47.

# The Brief

Plan a six-page booklet: two pieces of A4 paper folded in half give you six pages, with a front and back cover.

Choose five sculptors and write a profile of each one, thinking about what information your reader might want to know:

- When did the sculptor live?
- What materials did they like to use?
- Where can their work be seen?
- Why did they choose what they decided to sculpt?

- Find an image of your favourite piece of work for each artist and print it off for your booklet.
- Write a report–style caption for each image.
- Design a cover for the booklet.

You need to describe what is different about each sculptor.

Remember, 'report-style' means present tense! Where will you put the contents list for your booklet?

# Da Vinci Files

That's fantastic, I feel I know more about sculpture now, but I wonder why people sculpt rather than paint?
- For my challenge choose your own favourite sculptor.
- Research some more books or websites about their work so you can discover the answer to my query!
- Is there a difference betwen a sculpture and a statue?

# A sensory garden

Brain Academy has twinned with Strakely Special School. Some of the children there are physically disabled and love spending time in the open air.

Let's build them a fantastic garden, Da Vinci, so they have a lovely environment to go outside and enjoy!

Great idea, Bazza. Let's get to work!

## The Quest

Your quest is to develop a small area in the school grounds which is accessible for disabled children and their friends.
You must design a sensory garden, which has plenty of colour, smells, sounds and different textures to experience.

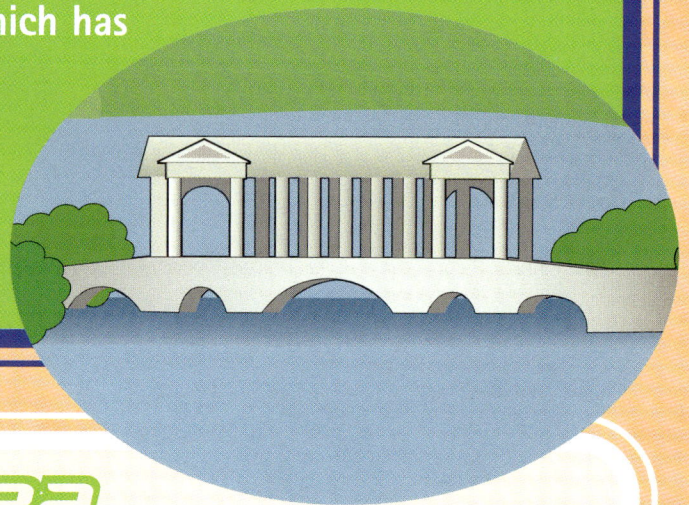

## Research Area

Try these sites to find out about sensory gardens:
http://www.rsdmanchester.org/facilities/garden.html
http://www.schoolsgarden.org.uk

There is more information on pages 46–47.

# The Brief

You will need to think about:

- Space – consider the size of the area you will need.
- Design – what kinds of areas are you going to include? For example, water features, lawns, etc.
- Access considerations – think about paths, garden furniture, slopes or steps.
- Plants – which plants will stimulate the senses? For example herbs, scented blossoms, mosses or palms.
- Suitable materials – will you use grass, gravel, paving stones, cobbles?
- Maybe you could include sculptures, art work, dovecotes or other features.

Design your garden using just one side of A4. Draw the space to scale and use captions to complete the design.

For children in wheelchairs think about the height of the plants by using raised flowerbeds.

Think about attracting birds, as they look and sound lovely!

# Da Vinci Files

Find out about the work of the National Trust and the kinds of gardens and facilities they provide for sensory impaired people.

- Try to visit one in your locality and then produce your own brochure explaining what it has to offer, or suggest ways in which its disabled access could be improved.
- For further details go to www.nationaltrust.org.uk

# Jurassic lark

Da Vinci, those D.A.F.T. agents have been trying to steal my collection of dinosaur fossils.

We need something to scare off those prehistoric pests and give them a monster fright.

## The Quest

Your quest is to build a model dinosaur with moving parts to scare off the DAFT agents.
The model must be pneumatic, which means controlled by air and Echo should be able to make it quickly using your instructions.

## Research Area

Look at this website to find out how dinosaurs moved:

http://dsc.discovery.com/stories/dinos/bbc/howdoweknow/q63.html

There is more information on pages 46–47.

# The Brief

Experiment making pneumatic systems. Use the following items.

- Washing-up bottles
- Syringes
- Card
- Masking tape
- Tubes
- Construction kits

**Explore how you can make something move using these items.**

Try fixing a balloon to a bottle using a 5mm tube.

Ask for help with making holes in your card.

# Da Vinci Files

Now it's time to build the dinosaur for Echo.
In order to scare off the thieves your dinosaur must:

- have moving parts, powered by air;
- look like a dinosaur.

Answer these questions first:

- What materials will you use?
- How big will your dinosaur be?
- Which parts will move and how?
- What will you need to do first?
- What will you name it?

13

# school dinners

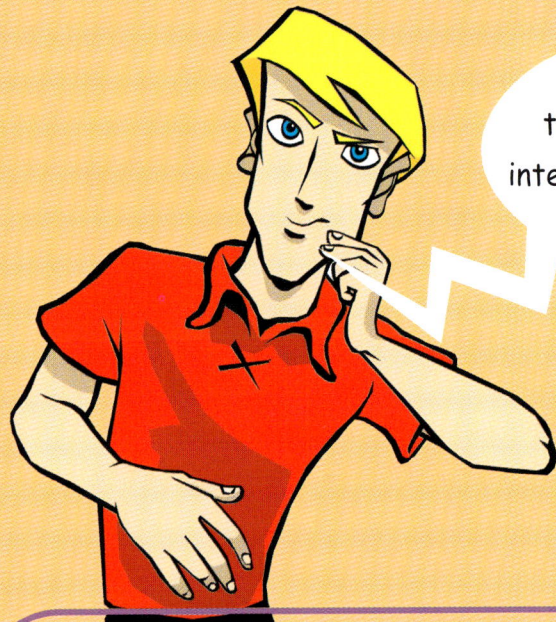

A challenge, sir! the School Council wants interesting school dinners for all the students.

The student population is made up of Christians, Hindus and Muslims, so they'd better do their research carefully.

## The Quest

As a member of the Brain Academy School Council, where members from all ethnic and religious backgrounds are represented, your task is to produce a choice of school dinner menus for a week. The menu needs to respect the diversity of religious and cultural differences and be healthy and interesting enough for us to want extra helpings!

## Research Area

Start by consulting Jamie Oliver and his healthy eating/healthy schools campaign.

http://www.feedmebetter.com

There is more information on pages 46–47.

# The Brief

Remember you must research:

- food that is acceptable on cultural and religious grounds to all represented groups;
- healthy food in all groups;
- ways to persuade different cultures to try new kinds of food.

Present your choice of menus:

- This should be in a chart form with THREE choices of main course, TWO desserts and a drink with water as a daily alternative.
- You don't need to specify suitability for each ethnic group, but make sure each group has at least one option.
- Graphics will make your menus look more eye-catching.

*I wonder which new foods the children will want to try.*

*How can you make vegetables sound like an interesting alternative to meat if you're not a vegetarian?*

# Da Vinci Files

Let's help the Brain Academy learn how to survey our demanding members!

- Conduct a survey in your school of who would be prepared to eat what.
- Then present this in table/chart form, using ICT, bar charts and graphs.
- Display your results in the school dining hall.

# 'Faith without works is dead'

Da Vinci, just what does it mean to love your neighbour, as the Bible tells Christians to do?

It's all about putting your faith into action by caring in practical ways for those who are homeless, poor, sick, in prison or suffering. The Salvation Army is a good example of that.

So, well worth finding out about them, then.

## The Quest

Your quest is to research the work of the Salvation Army in helping others and then prepare a list of questions you would like to either ask a school visiting officer from the Salvation Army or send online to http://www.thesalvol.uuhost.uk.uu.net/schools .

You must then organise a class display of the kinds of areas the Salvation Army works in, so that the Brain Academy can learn about this important group.

## Research Area

Try searching here for information about the Salvation Army:
http://www.request.org.uk

You could also visit your local Salvation Army citadel.
There is more information on pages 46–47.

# The Brief

These are the things you will need to include in the display:

- a brief history and the organisation of the Salvation Army;
- descriptions and pictures of the types of work the Salvation Army is involved in;
- any interesting artefacts you can collect, such as newsletters and posters;
- a suitable heading.

Also consider:

- how you will organise class members for their contributions;
- what materials you will need for display;
- how much of the work will be word processed.

Will you want to include any of the Salvation Army's music? This is an important part of their work.

How about including their badge?

# Da Vinci Files

Now research the life and work of the founder of the Salvation Army, William Booth, and make it into a PowerPoint presentation, which could then be included as part of the display.

- What do successful founders need to start their organisations?

# Move to the rhythm!

The police parade is out of step. That evil Dr Hood has messed up our march.

Never mind. We'll soon have you back on the beat, Buster.

Can you help the police march to the same tune?

## The Quest

Your quest is to create march rhythms to keep the police in step and get Buster's crew marching in time. Think about how a beat is made, by using your hands and feet topractise marching and keeping time as a group.

## Research Area

Look at this website to experiment with rhythms and sounds:

http://www.ngfl-cymru.org.uk/vtc-home/vtc-ks2-home/vtc-ks2-music-composing

You can also use any music software that you have available.
There is more information on pages 46–47.

# The Brief

- Create at least two different march rhythms that will give the police a strong beat to follow.
- Use different instruments and speeds.
- Think about how and when the police are likely to march. Will they be on parade or going to work?
- What do the police want people to feel when they see them marching?
- Can you write the rhythm down so that anyone can play it?
- Can you use a computer to program the march?

Use keyboards as well as the computer and percussion instruments when you are creating your rhythms.

# Da Vinci Files

Fantastic work! Buster's police force needs a bit more information though.

- Give each march rhythm a different melody so the police know which is which.
- Record your music using a microphone and experiment with changing the speed.

# Signs of faith

Da Vinci, the fish sign is a kind of badge for many Christians today, isn't it?

Hmm, that sounds interesting. I'm going to investigate this and see what else I can find out about religious signs. Come and join me, Questers!

Yes, Serena. But its history goes back a long way. In fact it used to be a secret sign.

## The Quest

1   Your quest is to find out about the significance of the fish sign for Christians.
    What other signs or symbols do they use?

2   What is the Star of David and why is it important for Jews? How was it used in World War II?
    Find other examples of signs in the Jewish faith.

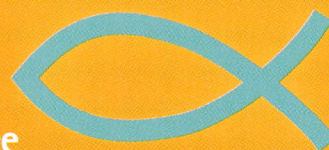

## Research Area

Look at the following website to find out about different signs in a variety of faiths:
http://www.reonline.org.uk

There is more information on pages 46–47.

# The Brief

Having done your internet research you will need to choose five different signs and symbols for both Christianity and Judaism.

- Where are they used?
- How are they used?
- What aspects of the religion does it tell you about?

Present your information as a non-chronological report.

Word-process it and use clip-art or import pictures from the internet as well to illustrate what you have discovered through your investigation.

Think about the layout of the information. Make it as clear as possible for the reader.

Caption the images to make it clear what people are looking at.

# Da Vinci Files

- Now you have completed your quest, take it a step further and design your own religious symbol or sign, using a computer graphics program.
- Include a brief written description about what it represents and its significance.

# Spilling the beans!

Everything in my allotment has been growing so slowly, Echo, I might just dig it over and make a football pitch instead...

Stop, Bazza! Growing your own veg is a great way to eat more organically. Let's get you back on track with something that shows quick results.

Well, the fastest veg I know is the runner bean. On your marks, get set, grow!

## The Quest

To help keep Prince Barrington motivated enough to keep growing organic veg, your quest is to grow as many runner beans as possible. Then write (very) clear instructions for Bazza so that he can grow beans all over the grounds of his mansion.

## Research Area

Look at this website to find out how to help plants grow well:

http://www.bbc.co.uk/schools/scienceclips/ages/7_8/plants_grow.shtml

There is more information on pages 46–47.

# The Brief

Design and carry out a fair test to see how much water runner bean plants prefer to have. This means growing the beans under two different sets of conditions to see which grow the fastest.

- Water one set of beans once a day.
- Water the second set of beans every other day.

You will need:
- Runner bean shoots
- Pots
- Measuring jug
- Water
- Light
- Soil

The more beans you get, the better the plant has done.

Try to make your test as fair as possible.

# Da Vinci Files

- Use the computer to keep a careful record of how much water you give each plant and how much it grows each week.
- Write a recommendation and some instructions for Prince Barrington about how much water a bean plant should be given to help it produce as many beans as possible.

# D-Day for the Dodont Bird

Da Vinci, a word in your shell-like. The egg of the Greater Spotted Dodont bird needs special protection. Its parents are egg-ceptionally worried.

Tell them not to beat themselves up over it. We'll scramble our brain cells and come up with a solution, Echo!

## The Quest

Your quest is to design and make a special package to safely transport the Dodont egg from the bird's parents to Echo's bird sanctuary at the Brain Academy. Remember, the package should be strong on the outside but soft on the inside to preserve that egg.

## Research Area

Find out about egg shells here:
http://www.theranger.co.uk/husbandry/hus4.htm

and egg cartons here:
http://www.eggboxes.com

There is more information on pages 46–47.

# The Brief

Collect suitable materials.

These will include:

- Paper
- Tape
- Cardboard
- Straws
- Cotton wool
- Anything else you feel would be useful

Now design your package.

The package needs to be strong and light to protect the egg and escape damage on its dangerous journey.

- What materials will you use?
- Where will the egg be placed?
- Draw your design.
- Can you improve your design?

# Da Vinci Files

Now it's time to build your package and get that egg back to the Brain Academy.
To be successful you will need to test it.

- Place an egg inside the package.
- Take it into the playground.
- Throw the package as high as you can.
- Well? Is your egg still in one piece?

# where shall we worship?

> If someone moved into our local area looking for a church to worship in, what would you suggest, Da Vinci?

> Research is the first step to making a good recommendation, Huxley! Let's get started!

## The Quest

You are going to investigate the range of different Christian religious buildings from a variety of denominations and research their particular features. Then you will use this information to compile a comparison chart for the newcomer, which outlines your findings about each church in a clear and easy to follow way.

## Research Area

Find out about Christian religious buildings here:
http://www.request.org.uk
http://www.educhurch.org.uk
You could ask your local church leaders to explain more about their church building.

There is more information on pages 46–47.

# The Brief

The websites will give you lots of information about the interior of different churches. You want to give your newcomer to the area as wide a range as possible to choose from. Look at those churches which offer the greatest contrast from each other.

Think about:

- Where each church is located.
- The architecture – compare the age, decoration and Christian symbols and religious objects for each building.
- Size – look at the layout of each building and how many people could fit in there.
- Do the objects differ or are many of the features the same in each church building?
- Is the church modern or old?
- What are your own impressions of each building?

Don't forget to look at the different denominations within the Christian church, not just Anglican buildings.

You could visit some local churches too and see for yourself!

# Da Vinci Files

- Find out the similarities and differences between Christian church buildings and a Hindu Temple or a Mosque.
- Prepare a five-minute talk about the buildings to give to your class.
- Share your information or work in groups with your Hindu and Muslim friends to explain your findings.
- www.reonline.org.uk will give a selection of sites where you can do some virtual tours for your research.

# Sandy's safety drill

I've found another school to 'twin' with the Brain Academy, but I need a lot of information about both schools so that I can be sure to protect them.

Great idea, Sandy, but what kind of information do you need about a school to keep it safe?

We have to think about how people get into and out of the building and where the water supplies are. Perhaps the Academy students can help.

## The Quest

Your quest is to design a questionnaire for a fire safety check for both schools. Work with a friend. When you have thought of the questions you want to ask (not more than six!) make a table with space for the answers. You can draw it, or create it on the computer.

## Research Area

Find out about safety here:
http://www.staywise.co.uk/activities

There is more information on pages 46–47.

# The Brief

You will need to investigate these points to prepare your questionnaire:

- Find out as much as you can about what to do if there was a fire.
- Ask to see the school's fire policy.
- Go round your school and note entrances, exits, and where the water supplies are.
- Where are the fire alarms? How do people know how to use them?

**FIRE**

Now write a six-question sheet and fill in the answers about your own school.

Send a copy to your contact at your twin school.

Collecting information will make you an expert! How will you make sure that other people know as much as you do?

Keep the questions short or people will get bored reading them!

# Da Vinci Files

Good work, Questers. It's now time to inform your school.
- Work out the best way of getting your information across.
- Will it be with posters, a talk in assembly or an entry on the school website?
- Who will you need to help you?

# A D.A.F.T. Nordic trick

There is a strange pattern to the latest D.A.F.T. raids. I can see from my historical maps that all of them happened in towns and cities where the Vikings once settled.

Top work, Serena! Now you will be able to predict where those D.A.F.T. agents will strike next and foil their Viking raids.

## The Quest

Your quest is to find out about the places in England and Scotland that were founded by the Viking invaders. Only by doing this will Serena be able to foil the D.A.F.T. agents. Find out about prefixes and suffixes which tell you that a place has Norse or Viking beginnings and plot them on a map.

## Research Area

This is a great starting place for researching the Vikings:

http://www.bbc.co.uk/history/ancient/vikings/

There is more information on pages 46–47.

# The Brief

**To make your own historical map, start by drawing a large outline of Great Britain on a poster-sized piece of paper.**

- **Study a modern map of Great Britain.**
- **Plot as many Viking settlements as you can on your map.**
- **Mark the place name and write what the name means.**
- **Add any interesting findings you may come across on your quest.**
- **Decorate the map in a Viking style.**

The suffix '-by' means homestead or village. So Grimsby means 'Grim's homestead' and Derby or Der-by means 'village by the deer'.

I think the suffix '-vik' means something too.

# Da Vinci Files

- Make up some Viking settlements of your own.
- They could be connected to your friends and family or features of your environment like buildings and rivers.
- Give your settlements suitable Viking names.

# Hedgehog Alert!

An amazing fact, Huxley! Hedgehogs form 29% of mammals killed on British roads each year.

That's a disaster for our prickly pals, Da Vinci. What can we do to help?

I know, we'll launch a 'Hedgehog Alert' campaign!

## The Quest

Questers, the Academy is near a busy main road and there have been several sightings recently of dead hedgehogs close by. You are going to start a campaign alerting people to the dangers for hedgehogs. You will need to advise everyone of the basic facts about hedgehog welfare and organisations that can help.

**STOP**

## Research Area

**Start your research here:**
http://www.software-technics.com/bhps/carers.html

There is more information on pages 46–47.

# The Brief

Your fact-file will need to include the essential information about where hedgehogs live and what they eat.
You will then need to provide information about:
- the daily risks that hedgehogs face;
- different organisations that exist to help in the preservation of hedgehogs;
- how individuals can help.

Remember that a campaign needs eye-catching material as well as factual information, so you could include:
- a slogan or logo on advertising material for a poster or badge;
- pictures from the internet.

Remember to divide your information into clear sections and make it easy and interesting to read so that people will be persuaded to help.

Use bullet points too; they get the info across and are quick to read!

# Da Vinci Files

Well done! Now design a small wildlife area for our Brain Academy which will both attract hedgehogs and provide a safe environment for them. Show your designs on an eye-catching poster to put up in the school hall.

# Singing sums!

Dr Hood and his D.A.F.T. agents are confusing the Maths trainees. They are stopping our amazing Mathematicians from learning their 7 times tables.

I know just how to turn the tables on them this time.

## The Quest

To help our trainees at the Brain Academy we need you to take part in this important task. Your quest is to make up a singing game to teach everyone the 7 times table.

## Research Area

Look at this website to experiment with rhythms and sounds:

http://www.multiplication.com/students.htm

There is more information on pages 46–47.

# The Brief

Create a rap that will help the Maths trainees learn the 7 times table.

- The rap should include the table in order and should then ask mixed-up Maths questions.

- Make the rap start slowly and gradually speed up.

- Think about the words that rhyme with the numbers in the 7 times table.

Keep the same musical pattern for each part of the table.

Make sure your song is easy to remember!

# Da Vinci Files

- Write down your composition clearly. Record it and evaluate how useful it is.

- Now adapt your rap for other tables that the trainees might find tricky to learn.

# The hills are alive at Brain Academy

We've got a whole group of Brain Academy students lost out on the hills. The only equipment they have is a magnet and a sewing kit. What use is that?

I know it's enough to get them home. Follow me...

## The Quest

Your quest is to help the group make a compass using just the equipment they have so they can work out the way back to base camp.

## Research Area

Look at this website to find out about making a compass. Write down two possible methods.

http://science.howstuffworks.com/compass2.htm

There is more information on pages 46–47.

# The Brief

- Use the equipment the group has to design and make a compass.
- Draw a diagram of your compass, first labelling all the pieces.
- Describe how the compass will work and then put the results of your test clearly into a table.

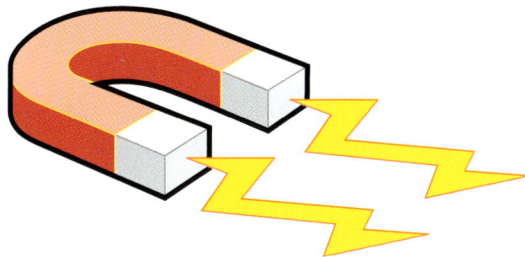

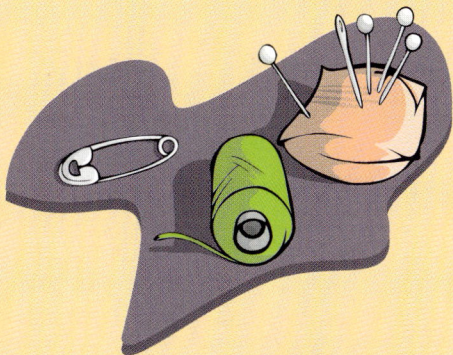

You need to test your design to be sure it will work.

Make sure your instructions are easy to understand — they can't be too bright if they managed to get lost!

# Da Vinci Files

Write a set of clear, easy to understand instructions to text to the lost team so we can get them home before nightfall. Well done, Questers!

# Read all about it!

We are drowning in newspapers, emails and news bulletins, Tex! Do you suppose this communications avalanche has been sent by those desperate D.A.F.T. agents?

Yes, I do! Dr Hood knows we need up-to-date information, but he's sent so much we can't cope! We need to sort the good info from the daily dross.

## The Quest

Your quest is to find out which medium – television, radio, newspaper or internet – is the best for each kind of news information.
This is vital for the Brain Academy and it will be useful for us to learn which are the most efficient routes to get the best information.

## Research Area

Newspapers: Collect one local paper, one of either *The Independent* or *The Times*, and a 'tabloid' such as the *Daily Mail* or *Daily Mirror*.
Television: Watch the evening news on any channel.
Radio: Listen to the news on the hour on Radio Four.
Internet: Go to http://news.bbc.co.uk

# The Brief

Over your research time, choose three stories in the news. One should be about the weather, one about some kind of disaster – an earthquake, perhaps, or a flood – and one 'human interest' story, perhaps about a celebrity.

Look at each story in all of the four different media listed in the research area. Give each medium a point on a scale of 1–10 for how it reports on each kind of story. Compare your findings with those of a friend.

- Which medium is best for information about the weather?
- Which gives the most useful information about disasters?
- Where can you get the best information on human interest stories?
- Which did you enjoy most?

Some stories don't appear at all on the radio news! Which ones are they?

You can spend a lot more time with a story when you are reading a newspaper!

# Da Vinci Files

When you have completed your research and made up your mind which is the best medium for each kind of story, write up your research for the Brain Academy.

- Write it as a brief recount (past tense) explaining how you did it in not more than 75 words.
- To make it quick and easy for the Academy to read, set out a table showing how many points each medium won for each kind of story. You can do this on the computer if you like.
- Can you recommend another news website?

# End of term at Brain Academy!

Hilary Kumar, the Prime Minister of our country, is on a secret mission. She wants to find a school which will be able to publish a special magazine. The magazine is called 'Extreme BA' and is all about young children who have helped Brain Academy in clever and interesting ways. The first edition will feature young Bobby Socks from Shoebury. He helped Buster Crimes solve the case of the 'leg of fish' recipe scandal that D.A.F.T. agents had spread around school canteens. Children were either too busy laughing or were too confused to eat their lunch. Bobby foiled the daft plans by stating that 'if fish could have fingers, why couldn't they have legs?' He was rewarded with the BA badge of honour from Da Vinci (via computer link of course).

Are you up to publishing 'Extreme BA'?

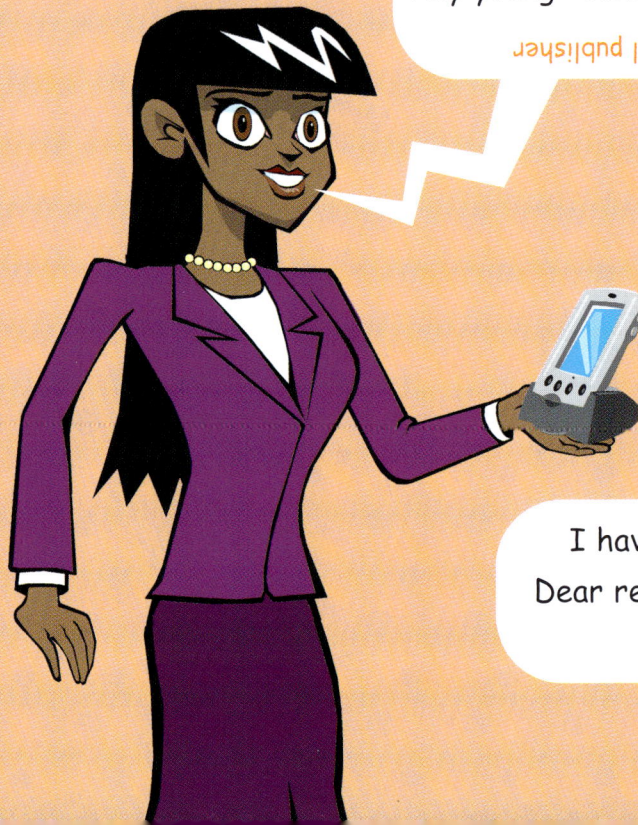

**NEWS**

Da Vinci, I need the best. Any young *Citizen Kane's out there?

*Famous fictional publisher

I have a school in mind. Dear reader, I'm thinking of ...YOU!

# Research Area

Gather together a collection of children's magazines and newspapers.

- How have the pictures and words been placed on the pages?
- What type of fonts (typefaces) have been used?
- What sort of colours have been used together?
- What captions and messages can you see?
- How is punctuation used for effect? Or letter size?

ouch

OOUUCCHHHH!!!!!

Have a look at these websites. They have been written in a 'magazine style'. There are lots of fun things to read and do!

http://www.cyberkids.com
http://www.timeforkids.com
http://www.globaleye.org.uk

- Using a computer, practise changing the fonts, sizes and colours of words and letters.
- Type the phrase 'Extreme Brain Academy'. How can you change the way it looks?
- Explore using clip-art and adding it to pieces of text.

CONTINUE ➡

# The Brief

Your brief is as follows:

To produce a magazine using images and text.

- It must show key events from your current year.

- It must include font and punctuation effects.

- Work in pairs.

- Assign one member of the team to be the Editor.

- Brainstorm the fun and exciting things that have happened at school.

- Decide who will be writing and presenting which key events.

- Prepare pieces of text which would benefit from a picture. For example, a description of the school.

- Ask your teacher how to find, retrieve and insert a graphic into a piece of text.

- Ask your teacher how to resize a graphic to fit onto a page if it is too small or too big.

- Experiment with fonts, text size, colour and punctuation.

- Access school/class photos which are digitally stored.

- Access school/class photos which have been printed.

# Da Vinci Files

You will need some or all of the following:
- Computer(s) and printer(s)
- Printer paper
- Digital camera
- A form of binding or presentation folder
- Artwork packages/clip-art

- You can work in pairs. One pair could produce a title page or front cover for the magazine. One pair could produce a back cover.

- Make sure each person has a turn at working with both the graphics and the text.

- Each pair must produce a graphic to match their text.

- Print the work out and bring all the pages together to form the magazine.

- In pairs and with your teacher, discuss the advantages of using ICT.

If you have made a great magazine, you may just get a call from me at the Academy!

# The TASC Problem Solving Wheel

## TASC: Thinking Actively in a Social Context

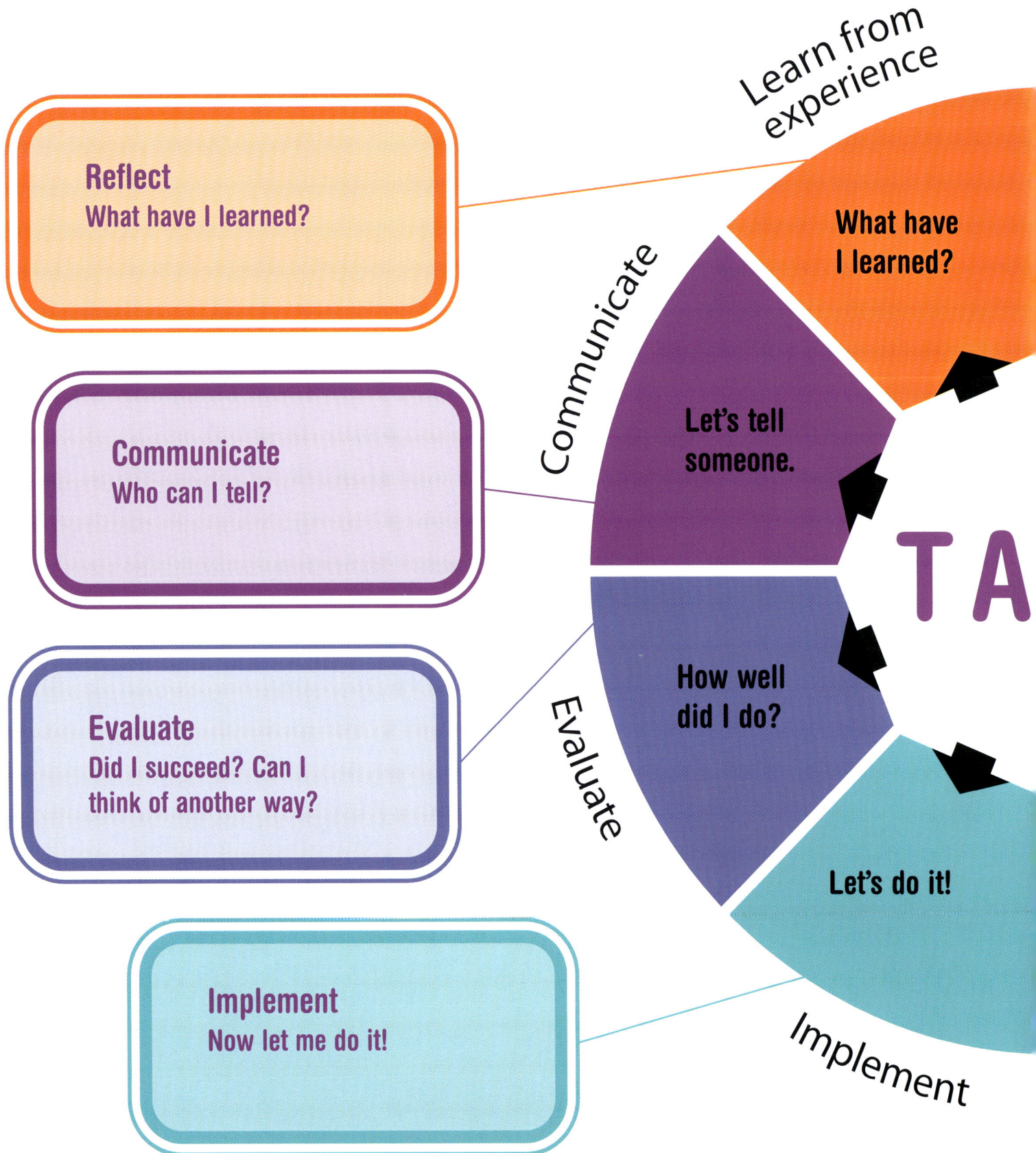

**Reflect**
What have I learned?

**Communicate**
Who can I tell?

**Evaluate**
Did I succeed? Can I
think of another way?

**Implement**
Now let me do it!

Learn from
experience

What have
I learned?

Communicate

Let's tell
someone.

How well
did I do?

Evaluate

Let's do it!

Implement

TA

We can learn to be expert thinkers!

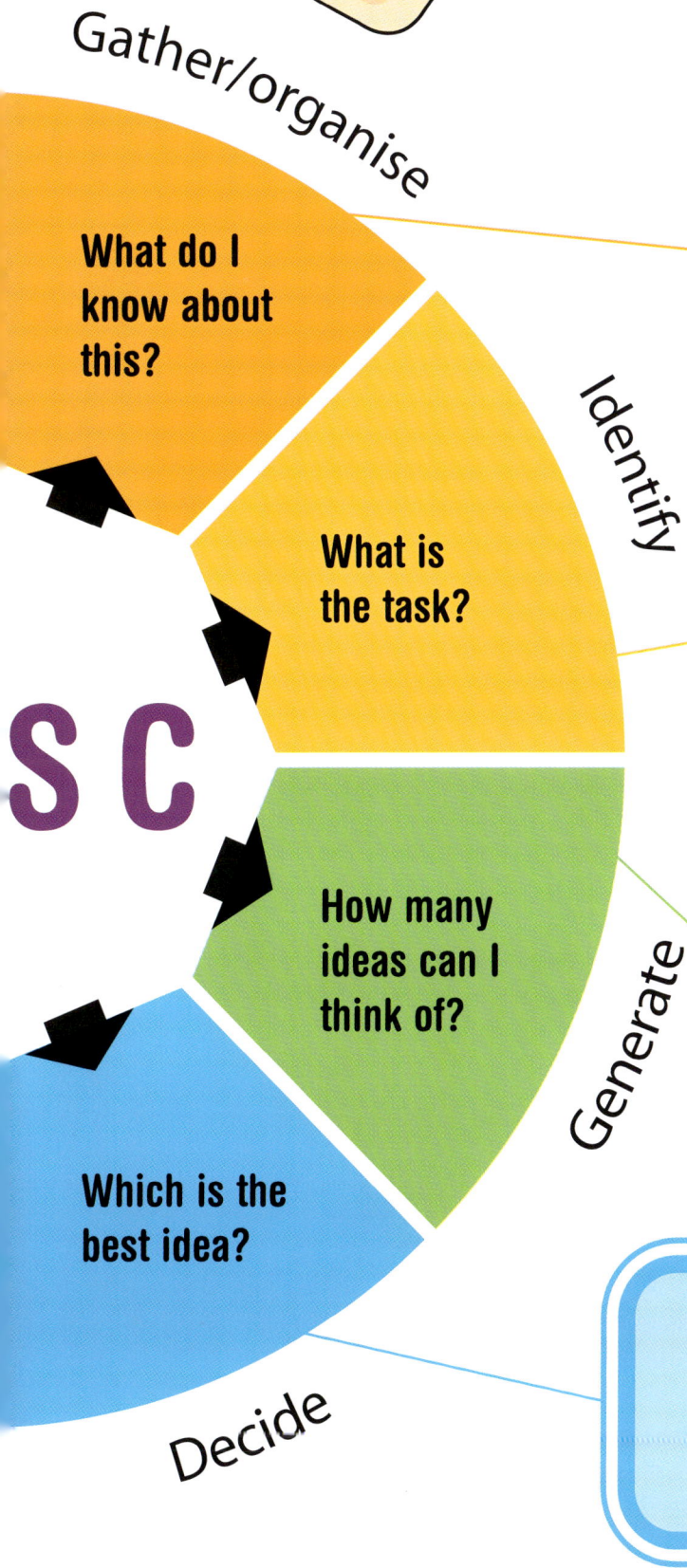

Gather/organise

What do I know about this?

Identify

What is the task?

S C

How many ideas can I think of?

Generate

Which is the best idea?

Decide

**Gather/organise**
What do I already know about this?

**Identify**
What am I trying to do?

**Generate**
How many ways can I do this?

**Decide**
Which is the best way?